Who's at the Seashore?

Written and Illustrated by
JOHN HIMMELMAN

NORTHWORD

Published by Taylor Trade Publishing
Lanham • New York • Boulder • Toronto • Plymouth, UK

Books for Young Readers

Published by Taylor Trade Publishing
An imprint of The Rowman & Littlefield Publishing Group, Inc.
4501 Forbes Boulevard, Suite 200, Lanham, Maryland 20706
www.rlpgtrade.com

Estover Road, Plymouth PL6 7PY, United Kingdom

Distributed by NATIONAL BOOK NETWORK

Designed by Lois A. Rainwater

Library of Congress Cataloging-in-Publication Data

Himmelman, John.
Who's at the seashore? / written and illustrated by John Himmelman.
p. cm.
ISBN-13: 978-1-58979-387-3 (cloth : alk. paper)
ISBN-10: 1-58979-387-0 (cloth : alk. paper)
1. Seashore animals—Juvenile literature. I. Title.
QL122.2.H564 2009
591.769'9—dc22   2008038264

Printed in China

To the kids
who helped me comb the beach
for sandhoppers.

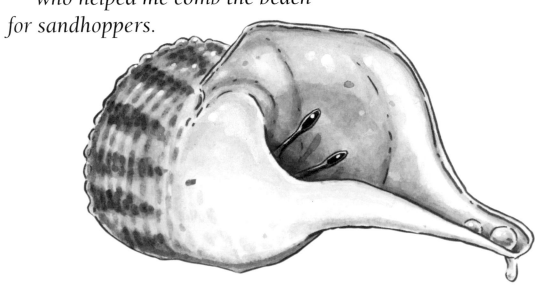

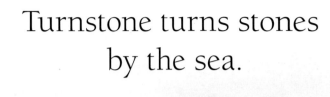

Turnstone turns stones
by the sea.

Ring-billed gull watches,
quietly.

Gull chases
when sand hopper hops.

Moon snail wiggles by
and stops.

Moon snail lays eggs
in the sand.

Horsefly finds
a place to land.

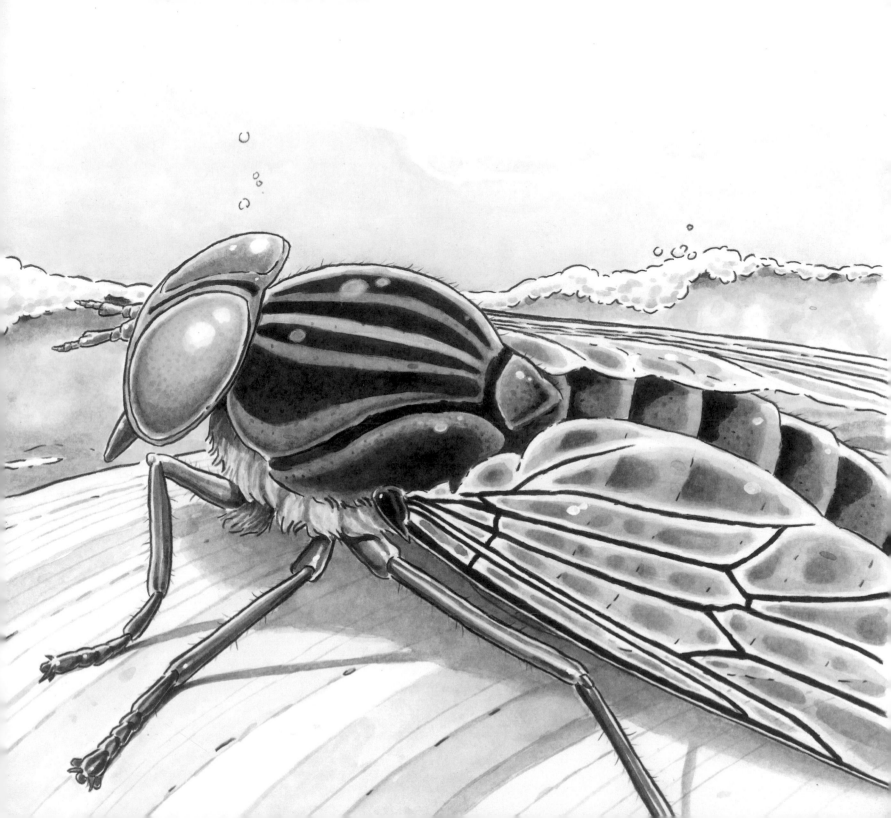

Horsefly flies
as the tide comes in.

Killifish swim,
fin to fin.

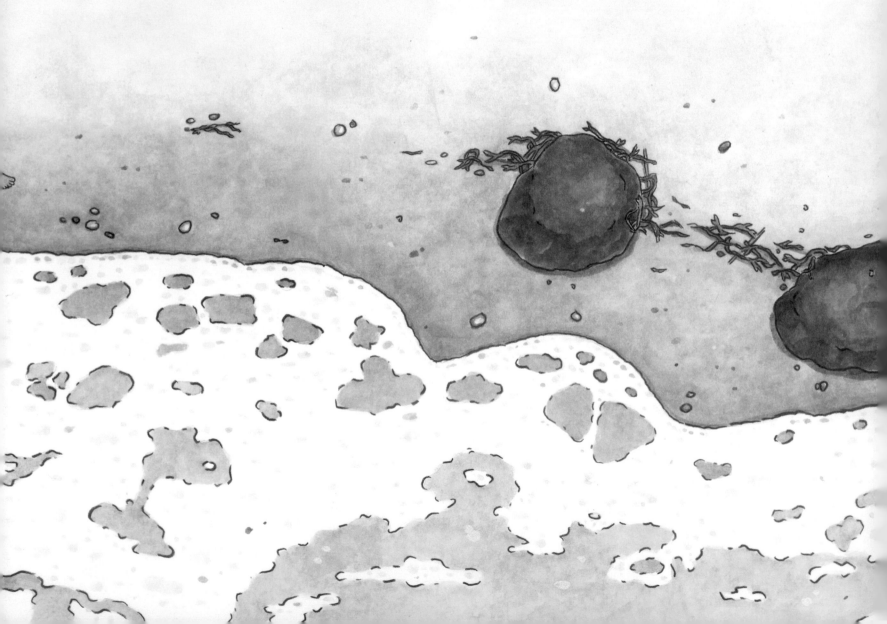

Killifish trapped
in a pool.

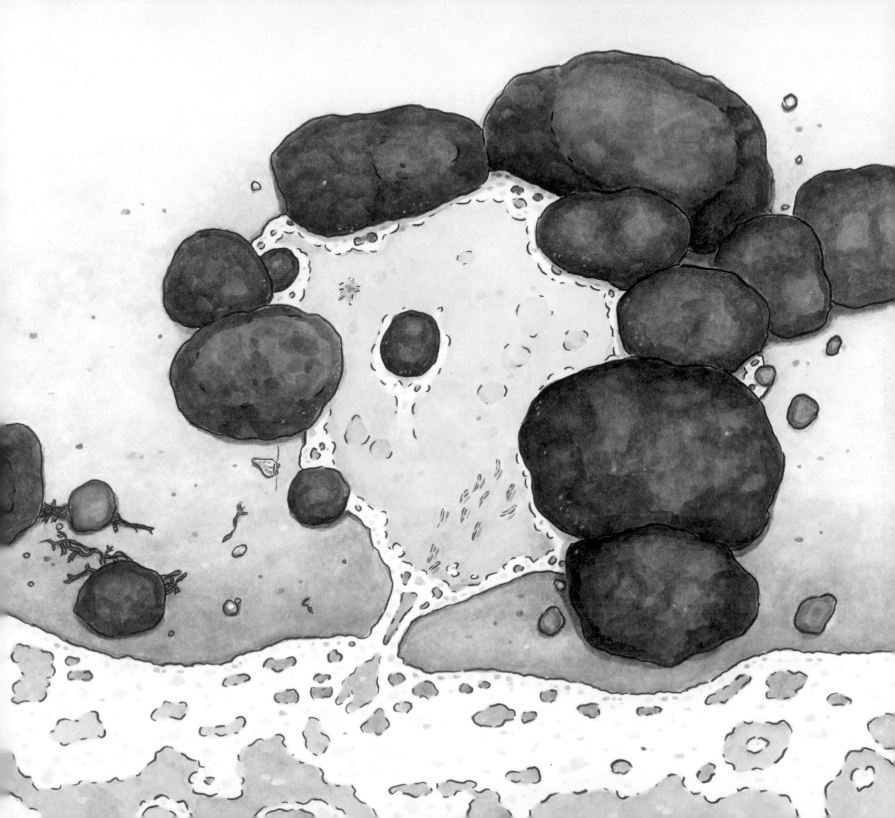

Hermit crab joins them
to get cool.

Hermit crab hides
from a curious eye.

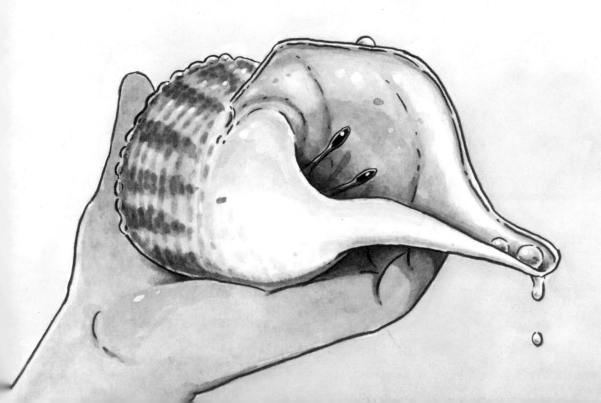

Sea star hunts
for clams nearby.

Two birds land, quietly.

Turnstone turns stones
by the sea.

Who's at the Seashore?

TURNSTONE - A turnstone is a type of shore bird. It hunts for insects and small creatures by flipping rocks and shells with its bill. We have two different kinds of turnstones in North America. The bird in this story is a ruddy turnstone.

RING-BILLED GULL - This bird is named for the dark ring around its bill. Like most gulls, they are good flyers, good swimmers, and good runners. They feed on a very wide variety of food.

SAND HOPPER - Sand hoppers are also known as beach fleas, but they are more closely related to shrimp. They live in the beach sand, where they feed on seaweed.

MOON SNAIL - Moon snails are shelled animals called mollusks that feed on other mollusks. They drill holes through the shells to get to their food. Their eggs are laid within a circular ribbon of sand and mucus. This is called a sand collar.

HORSEFLY - Horseflies are found in many different habitats, including beaches. The females have a saw-like mouthpart that draws blood from mammals. The blood helps her lay many eggs. The males feed on nectar and do not bite.

KILLIFISH - Also known as mummichog, killifish gather in tide pools and creeks in saltwater marshes. They feed on a variety of aquatic plants and animals.

HERMIT CRAB - Crabs are called crustaceans, which means they have their skeletons on the outside of their bodies. On most crabs, that shell is hard, but hermit crabs have soft shells and must use the discarded shells of mollusks. As they grow larger, they seek out new shells to protect their soft bodies. The hermit crab in this story is living in a whelk shell.

SEA STAR - Many call them starfish, but sea star is a better name, since they are not fish at all. Most have five legs. If one loses a leg, it will grow back. Sometimes it will grow back more legs than it lost! Sea stars eat mollusks. They pry open the shells with their strong arms.

CLAM - A clam is a mollusk that many of us, like the sea star in this story, have eaten! There are many different kinds of mollusks. Clams are called bivalves. This means that their soft body is protected between two hard shells.